The BRAZILIAN MASTERS 2nd Edition

ISBN 978-0-634-02408-5

HAL•LEONARD®
CORPORATION

7777 W. BLUEMOUND RD. P.O. BOX 13819 MILWAUKEE, WI 53213

Visit Hal Leonard Online at
www.halleonard.com

INTRODUCTION

There is no music more naturally suited to the guitar than Brazilian popular songs. The universal appeal of the music itself and the popularity of the guitar as an instrument join to make the bossa nova a favorite guitar style throughout the world.

It is not surprising that Brazilian music is so natural to the guitar when one discovers just how important the instrument is in Brazil and to her best composers. Antonio Carlos Jobim, one of the world's most popular songwriters, composes on both guitar and piano. Luiz Bonfá and Baden Powell, authors of many international hits, are both virtuoso soloists on the guitar. And there is something in the intimate sound of the instrument itself that lends perfectly to the subtle syncopations of *samba* and *bossa nova*.

This book has been designed not only to give pleasure to guitarists from average to expert playing ability, but also to serve as a method through which a player can learn the Brazilian style and gain enough understanding of it to arrange, compose, and improvise his or her own musical ideas within it. Going through the book will improve your reading as well as your techniques and musical expression.

Perhaps the greatest difficulty for players not familiar with the style is to get the "Brazilian swing." The following rhythm patterns contain most of the elements upon which this feeling is based. You can observe from the examples that the more complicated patterns are merely combinations of the basic ones. Play the basic examples until they feel natural and then go to the more difficult ones. Then as you go through the songs you will find it much easier to understand how they are to be played.

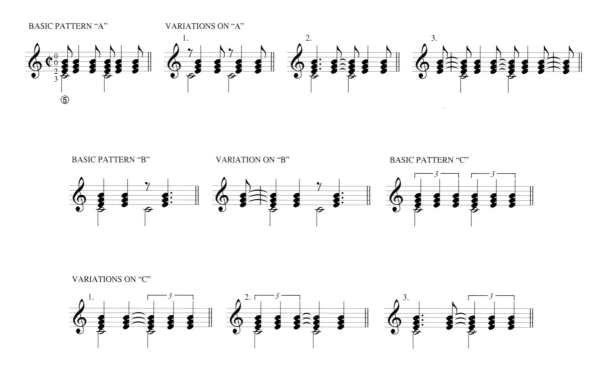

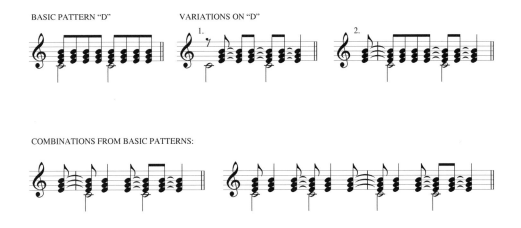

Another important thing to remember is that the basic beat is almost always a "two feel". (Note that most of the 4/4 pieces are marked in cut time ¢ and have two half notes per measure in the bass making for a 2/2 feel.) The bass is usually on the beat, but the melody is often on the off beats. If some of these more syncopated passages give you problems, try playing the melody and the chord part un-syncopated first and then anticipate the melody part until it makes sense musically as it is written. That plus listening to the original recordings should help you acquire a natural feel for the music.

Should you find the rhythm (A) difficult, first simplify it to (B) and then anticipate chord 1 of B before your thumb plays the bass note and extend chord 3 of B and extra 8th beat.

As with any music you wish to learn correctly, study the difficult passages slowly and thoroughly until they are "under your hands." Feel free to change the fingerings if you find a better way. Those given here follow the patterns typical of Brazilian players and can be useful for your own arranging, composing, or improvising.

In this collection there is a lot of variety of mood and feeling. So in each piece you learn, try to understand its mood and emphasize it as you play. By paying attention to the feeling and technical aspects of each piece you will grow both as a musician and guitarist.

DESAFINADO

Original Text by NEWTON MENDONÁA
Music by ANTONIO CARLOS JOBIM

EBONY SAMBA
(Sambanegro)

Music by LUIZ BONFÁ
and MARIA TOLEDO

Moderato (♩ = 60)

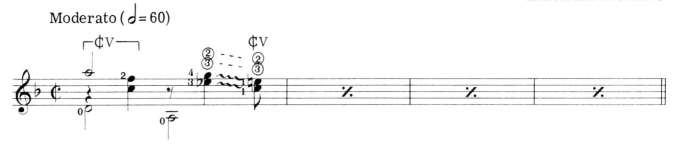

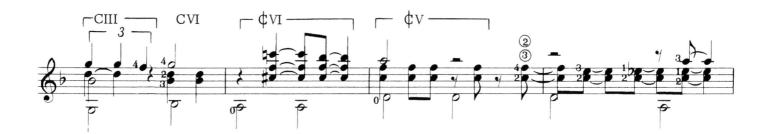

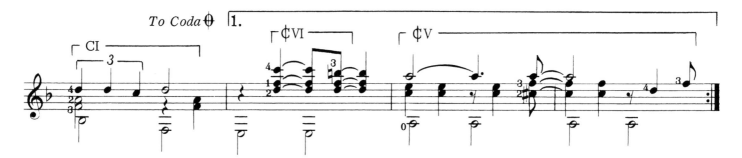

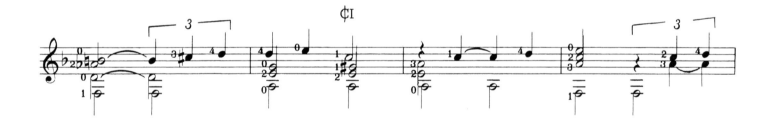

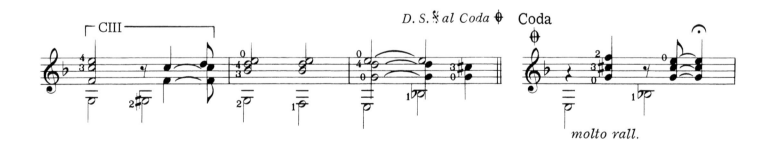

ENGANO

By ANTONIO CARLOS JOBIM
and LUIZ BONFÁ

Largo, con molto rubato

11

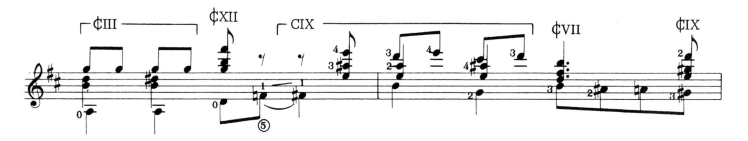

D. S. % al Coda ⊕

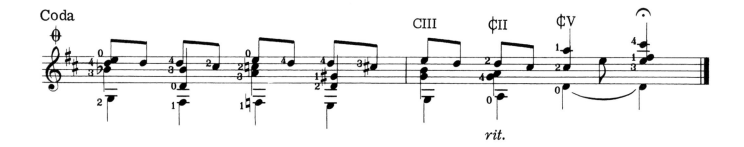

rit.

ILHA DE CORAL
(Coral Island)

By LUIZ BONFÁ

Moderato, con rubato

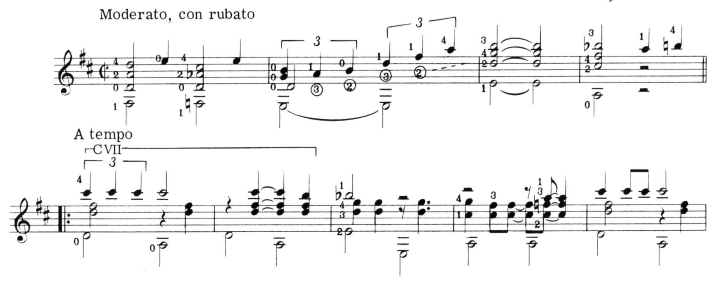

A tempo

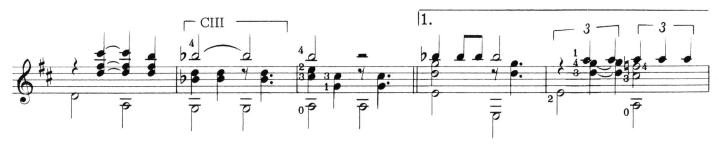

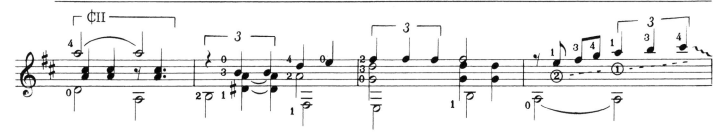

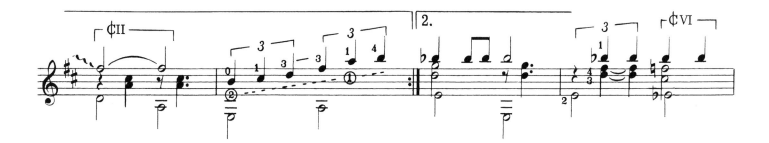

molto rit.

ESPERANÇA PERDIDA

By ANTONIO CARLOS JOBIM
and BILLY BLANCO

Largo, con poco rubato

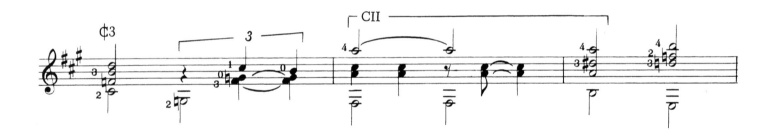

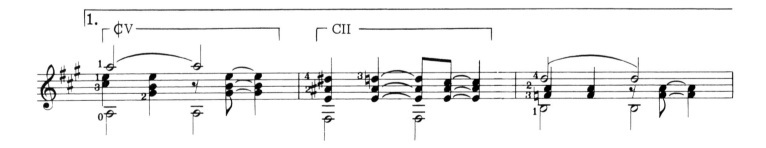

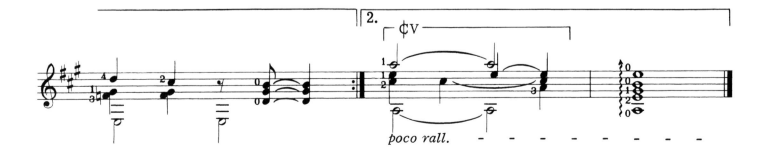

poco rall.

INCERTEZA
(I Always Knew)

By ANTONIO CARLOS JOBIM
and NEWTON MENDONÇA

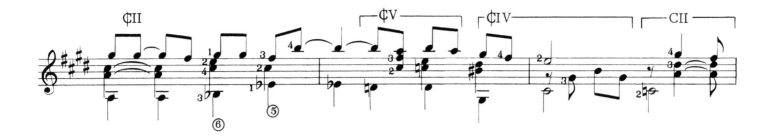

cresc. – – – – – – – – – – – – –

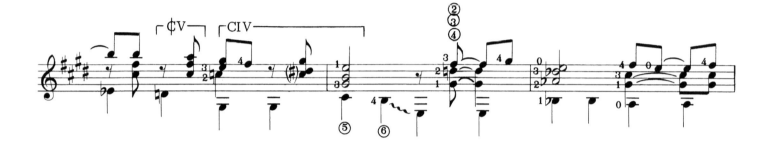

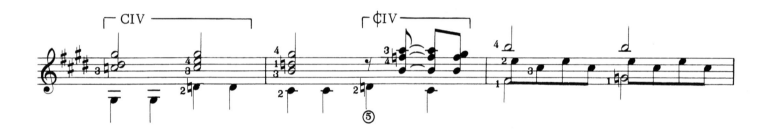

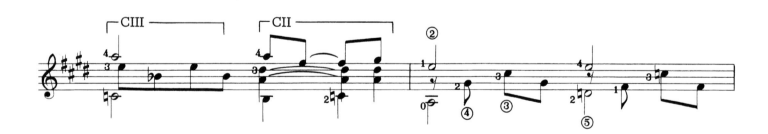

rall. - - - - - - - *molto rall.* - - - - - - - -

SAMBALAMENTO

By LUIZ BONFÁ

Moderato
(Repeat four times)

Repeat and fade

LITTLE BOAT

Original Lyric by RONALDO BOSCOLI
English Lyric by BUDDY KAYE
Music by ROBERTO MENESCAL

Moderato

MANHÃ DE CARNAVAL
(A Day in the Life of a Fool)

Words by CARL SIGMAN
Music by LUIZ BONFÁ

meno mosso   *p* *i* *m* *a* *p* *i* *m* *a* *m* *i*   poco rit.

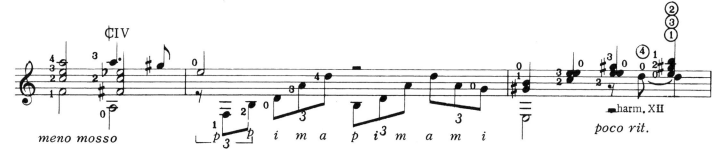

sustain chord   harm. XII

rit. - - - - - - - -

SAMBA DE DUAS NOTAS
(Two Note Samba)

Music by LUIZ BONFÁ
and MARIA TOLEDO

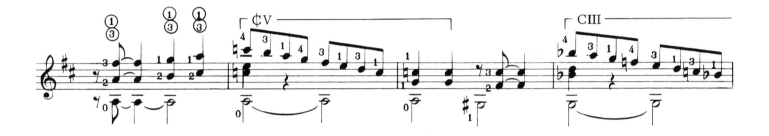

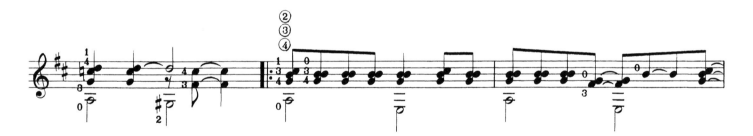

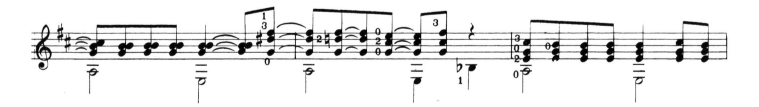

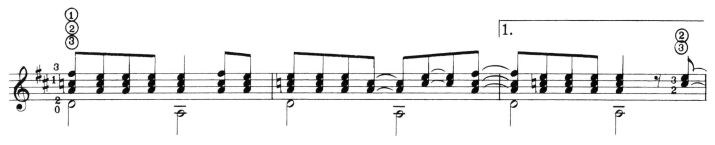

SAMBA TRISTE

By BILLY BLANCO
and BADEN POWELL

Lento to allegretto, *con rubato*

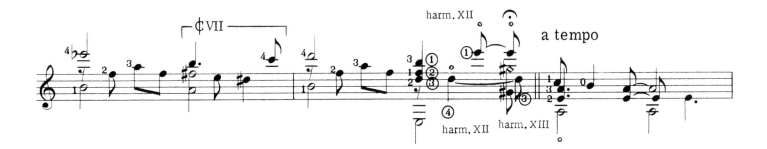

cresc. - - - - - - - - -

poco rit.

SE TODOS FOSSEM IGUAIS Á VOCÊ
(Someone to Light Up My Life)

Words and Music by ANTONIO CARLOS JOBIM
and VINICIUS DE MORAES

Largo, appassionato

poco rit.

più mosso

sustain

rit.

cresc. poco a poco - - - - - - - - - -

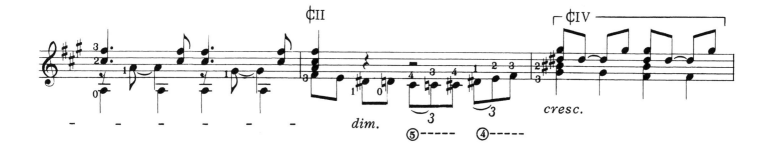

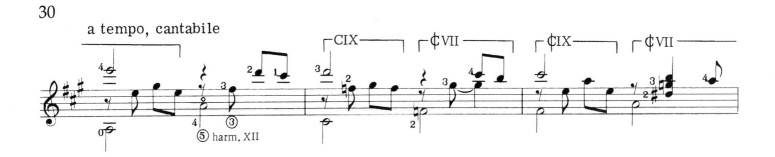

a tempo, cantabile

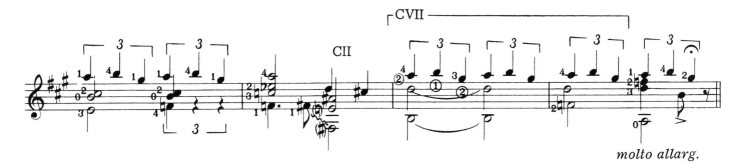

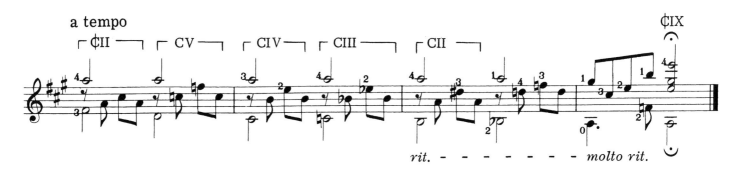

SOLIDÃO

By ANTONIO CARLOS JOBIM
and ALCIDES FERNANDES

Lento, con rubato

poco rit.

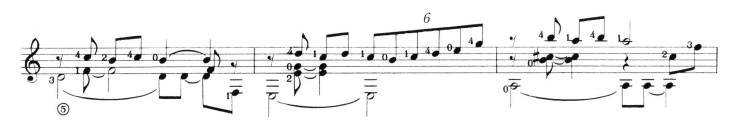

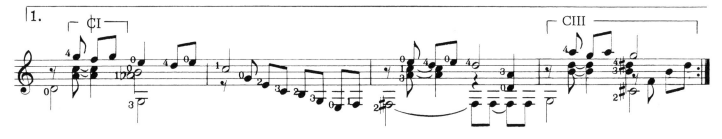

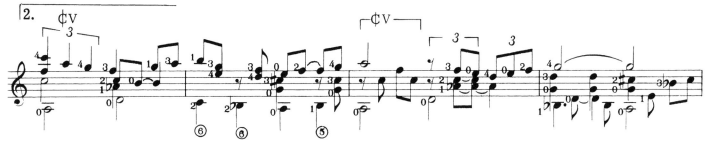

To Coda

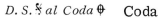

D. S. al Coda   Coda

poco rit.   molto rit.

SILENCIO DO AMOR
(The Silence of Love)

By LUIZ BONFÁ
and MARIA TOLEDO

Lento, con rubato

poco allarg.

a tempo moderato

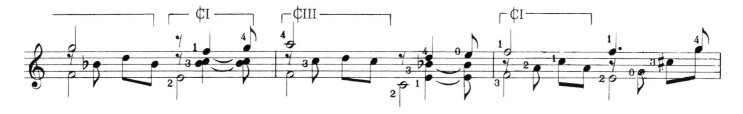

SO NICE
(Summer Samba)

Original Words and Music by
MARCOS VALLE and PAULO SERGIO VALLE
English Words by NORMAN GIMBEL

Drop D tuning:
(low to high) D-A-D-G-B-E

Moderato

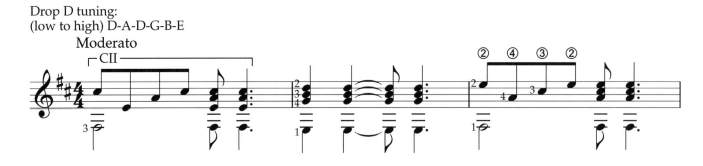

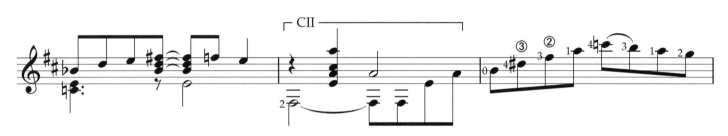

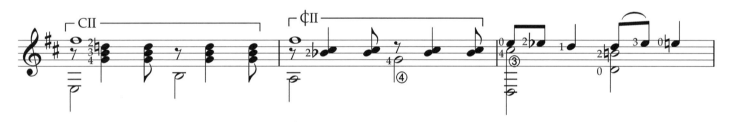

rit. - - - - - - - - - - - - - - - -

SAMBA DO AVIÃO

from the film COPACABANA PALACE

Words and Music by
ANTONIO CARLOS JOBIM

Rubato

A tempo: Moderato

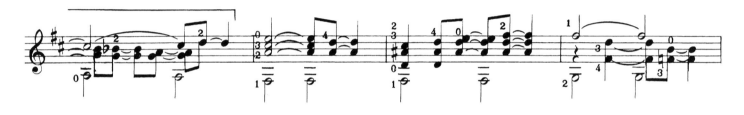

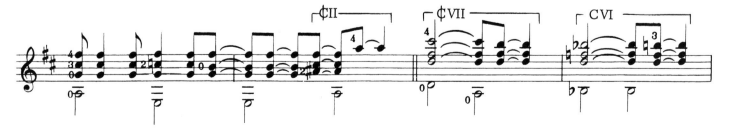

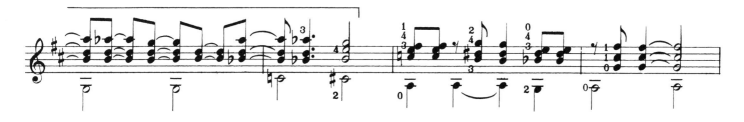

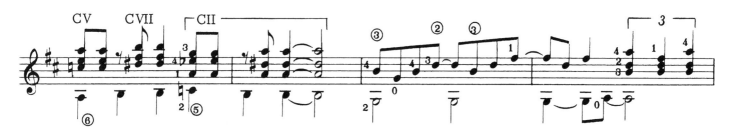

FINGERPICKING GUITAR BOOKS

Hone your fingerpicking skills with these great songbooks featuring solo guitar arrangements in standard notation and tablature. The arrangements in these books are carefully written for intermediate-level guitarists. Each song combines melody and harmony in one superb guitar fingerpicking arrangement. Each book also includes an introduction to basic fingerstyle guitar.

   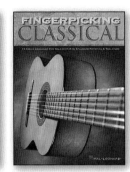 

Fingerpicking Acoustic
00699614 15 songs......................$14.99

Fingerpicking Acoustic Classics
00160211 15 songs......................$16.99

Fingerpicking Acoustic Hits
00160202 15 songs......................$15.99

Fingerpicking Acoustic Rock
00699764 14 songs......................$16.99

Fingerpicking Ballads
00699717 15 songs......................$15.99

Fingerpicking Beatles
00699049 30 songs......................$24.99

Fingerpicking Beethoven
00702390 15 pieces.....................$10.99

Fingerpicking Blues
00701277 15 songs $12.99

Fingerpicking Broadway Favorites
00699843 15 songs......................$9.99

Fingerpicking Broadway Hits
00699838 15 songs......................$7.99

Fingerpicking Campfire
00275964 15 songs......................$14.99

Fingerpicking Celtic Folk
00701148 15 songs......................$12.99

Fingerpicking Children's Songs
00699712 15 songs......................$9.99

Fingerpicking Christian
00701076 15 songs......................$12.99

Fingerpicking Christmas
00699599 20 carols.....................$12.99

Fingerpicking Christmas Classics
00701695 15 songs......................$7.99

Fingerpicking Christmas Songs
00171333 15 songs......................$10.99

Fingerpicking Classical
00699620 15 pieces.....................$10.99

Fingerpicking Country
00699687 17 songs......................$12.99

Fingerpicking Disney
00699711 15 songs......................$17.99

Fingerpicking Early Jazz Standards
00276565 15 songs $14.99

Fingerpicking Duke Ellington
00699845 15 songs......................$9.99

Fingerpicking Enya
00701161 15 songs......................$16.99

Fingerpicking Film Score Music
00160143 15 songs......................$15.99

Fingerpicking Gospel
00701059 15 songs......................$9.99

Fingerpicking Hit Songs
00160195 15 songs......................$12.99

Fingerpicking Hymns
00699688 15 hymns $12.99

Fingerpicking Irish Songs
00701965 15 songs......................$10.99

Fingerpicking Italian Songs
00159778 15 songs......................$12.99

Fingerpicking Jazz Favorites
00699844 15 songs......................$14.99

Fingerpicking Jazz Standards
00699840 15 songs......................$12.99

Fingerpicking Elton John
00237495 15 songs......................$15.99

Fingerpicking Latin Favorites
00699842 15 songs......................$12.99

Fingerpicking Latin Standards
00699837 15 songs......................$17.99

Fingerpicking Love Songs
00699841 15 songs......................$14.99

Fingerpicking Love Standards
00699836 15 songs $9.99

Fingerpicking Lullabyes
00701276 16 songs.......................$9.99

Fingerpicking Movie Music
00699919 15 songs......................$14.99

Fingerpicking Mozart
00699794 15 pieces.....................$10.99

Fingerpicking Pop
00699615 15 songs......................$14.99

Fingerpicking Popular Hits
00139079 14 songs......................$12.99

Fingerpicking Praise
00699714 15 songs......................$14.99

Fingerpicking Rock
00699716 15 songs......................$14.99

Fingerpicking Standards
00699613 17 songs......................$15.99

Fingerpicking Worship
00700554 15 songs......................$15.99

Fingerpicking Neil Young – Greatest Hits
00700134 16 songs......................$17.99

Fingerpicking Yuletide
00699654 16 songs......................$12.99

HAL•LEONARD®

Order these and more great publications from your favorite music retailer at

halleonard.com

Prices, contents and availability subject to change without notice.

CLASSICAL GUITAR

INSTRUCTIONAL BOOKS & METHODS AVAILABLE FROM HAL LEONARD

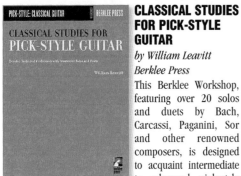

CLASSICAL STUDIES FOR PICK-STYLE GUITAR

by William Leavitt
Berklee Press

This Berklee Workshop, featuring over 20 solos and duets by Bach, Carcassi, Paganini, Sor and other renowned composers, is designed to acquaint intermediate to advanced pick-style guitarists with some of the excellent classical music that is adaptable to pick-style guitar. With study and practice, this workshop will increase a player's knowledge and proficiency on this formidable instrument.

50449440...$14.99

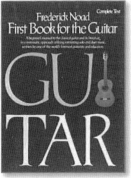

ÉTUDES SIMPLES FOR GUITAR

by Leo Brouwer
Editions Max Eschig

This new, completely revised and updated edition includes critical commentary and performance notes. Each study is accompanied by an introduction that illustrates its principal musical features and technical objectives, complete with suggestions and preparatory exercises.

50565810 Book/CD Pack........................$26.99

FIRST BOOK FOR THE GUITAR

by Frederick Noad
G. Schirmer, Inc.

A beginner's manual to the classical guitar. Uses a systematic approach using the interesting solo and duet music written by Noad, one of the world's foremost guitar educators. No musical knowledge is necessary. Student can progress by simple stages. Many of the exercises are designed for a teacher to play with the students. Will increase student's enthusiasm, therefore increasing the desire to take lessons.

50334370 Part 1......................................$14.99
50334520 Part 2......................................$18.99
50335160 Part 3......................................$16.99
50336760 Complete Edition....................$32.99

HAL LEONARD CLASSICAL GUITAR METHOD

by Paul Henry

This comprehensive and easy-to-use beginner's guide uses the music of the master composers to teach you the basics of the classical style and technique. Includes pieces by Beethoven, Bach, Mozart, Schumann, Giuliani, Carcassi, Bathioli, Aguado, Tarrega, Purcell, and more. Includes all the basics plus info on PIMA technique, two- and three-part music, time signatures, key signatures, articulation, free stroke, rest stroke, composers, and much more.

00697376 Book/Online Audio (no tab)................$16.99
00142652 Book/Online Audio (with tab)............$17.99

A MODERN APPROACH TO CLASSICAL GUITAR

by Charles Duncan

This multi-volume method was developed to allow students to study the art of classical guitar within a new, more contemporary framework. For private, class or self-instruction.

00695114 Book 1 – Book Only..............................$8.99
00695113 Book 1 – Book/Online Audio................$12.99
00699204 Book 1 – Repertoire Book Only............$11.99
00699205 Book 1 – Repertoire Book/Online Audio .$16.99
00695116 Book 2 – Book Only..............................$8.99
00695115 Book 2 – Book/Online Audio................$12.99
00699208 Book 2 – Repertoire.............................$12.99
00365530 Book 3 – Book/Online Audio................$14.99
00695119 Composite Book/CD Pack....................$32.99

100 GRADED CLASSICAL GUITAR STUDIES

Selected and Graded by Frederick Noad

Frederick Noad has selected 100 studies from the works of three outstanding composers of the classical period: Sor, Giuliani, and Carcassi. All these studies are invaluable for developing both right hand and left hand skills. Students and teachers will find this book invaluable for making technical progress. In addition, they will build a repertoire of some of the most melodious music ever written for the guitar.

14023154...$29.99

CHRISTOPHER PARKENING GUITAR METHOD

THE ART & TECHNIQUE OF THE CLASSICAL GUITAR

Guitarists will learn basic classical technique by playing over 50 beautiful classical pieces, 26 exercises and 14 duets, and through numerous photos and illustrations. The method covers: rudiments of classical technique, note reading and music theory, selection and care of guitars, strategies for effective practicing, and much more!

00696023 Book 1/Online Audio $22.99
00695228 Book 1 (No Audio) $17.99
00696024 Book 2/Online Audio $22.99
00695229 Book 2 (No Audio) $17.99

SOLO GUITAR PLAYING

by Frederick M. Noad

Solo Guitar Playing can teach even the person with no previous musical training how to progress from simple single-line melodies to mastery of the guitar as a solo instrument. Fully illustrated with diagrams, photographs, and over 200 musical exercises and repertoire selections, these books offer instruction in every phase of classical guitar playing.

14023147 Book 1/Online Audio $34.99
14023153 Book 1 (Book Only)............................$24.99
14023151 Book 2 (Book Only) $19.99

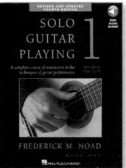

TWENTY STUDIES FOR THE GUITAR

ANDRÉS SEGOVIA EDITION

by Fernando Sor
Performed by Paul Henry

20 studies for the classical guitar written by Beethoven's contemporary, Fernando Sor, revised, edited and fingered by the great classical guitarist Andres Segovia. These essential repertoire pieces continue to be used by teachers and students to build solid classical technique. Features 50-minute demonstration audio.

00695012 Book/Online Audio $22.99
00006363 Book Only..$11.99

HAL•LEONARD®

Order these and more publications
from your favorite music retailer at
halleonard.com

Prices, contents and availability subject to change without notice.

0523
005

HAL•LEONARD GUITAR PLAY-ALONG

Complete song lists available online.

This series will help you play your favorite songs quickly and easily. Just follow the tab and listen to the audio to the hear how the guitar should sound, and then play along using the separate backing tracks. Audio files also include software to slow down the tempo without changing pitch. The melody and lyrics are included in the book so that you can sing or simply follow along.

INCLUDES TAB

VOL. 1 – ROCK ....00699570 / $17.99
VOL. 2 – ACOUSTIC ....00699569 / $17.99
VOL. 3 – HARD ROCK ....00699573 / $19.99
VOL. 4 – POP/ROCK ....00699571 / $16.99
VOL. 5 – THREE CHORD SONGS ....00300985 / $16.99
VOL. 6 – '90S ROCK ....00298615 / $16.99
VOL. 7 – BLUES ....00699575 / $19.99
VOL. 8 – ROCK ....00699585 / $16.99
VOL. 9 – EASY ACOUSTIC SONGS ....00151708 / $16.99
VOL. 11 – EARLY ROCK ....00699579 / $17.99
VOL. 12 – ROCK POP ....00291724 / $17.99
VOL. 14 – BLUES ROCK ....00699582 / $17.99
VOL. 15 – R&B ....00699583 / $17.99
VOL. 16 – JAZZ ....00699584 / $17.99
VOL. 17 – COUNTRY ....00699588 / $17.99
VOL. 18 – ACOUSTIC ROCK ....00699577 / $15.95
VOL. 20 – ROCKABILLY ....00699580 / $17.99
VOL. 21 – SANTANA ....00174525 / $19.99
VOL. 22 – CHRISTMAS ....00699600 / $15.99
VOL. 23 – SURF ....00699635 / $17.99
VOL. 24 – ERIC CLAPTON ....00699649 / $19.99
VOL. 25 – THE BEATLES ....00198265 / $19.99
VOL. 26 – ELVIS PRESLEY ....00699643 / $17.99
VOL. 27 – DAVID LEE ROTH ....00699645 / $16.95
VOL. 29 – BOB SEGER ....00699647 / $16.99
VOL. 30 – KISS ....00699644 / $17.99
VOL. 32 – THE OFFSPRING ....00699653 / $14.95
VOL. 33 – ACOUSTIC CLASSICS ....00699656 / $19.99
VOL. 35 – HAIR METAL ....00699660 / $19.99
VOL. 36 – SOUTHERN ROCK ....00699661 / $19.99
VOL. 37 – ACOUSTIC UNPLUGGED ....00699662 / $22.99
VOL. 39 – '80s METAL ....00699664 / $17.99
VOL. 40 – INCUBUS ....00699668 / $17.95
VOL. 41 – ERIC CLAPTON ....00699669 / $17.99
VOL. 42 – COVER BAND HITS ....00211597 / $16.99
VOL. 43 – LYNYRD SKYNYRD ....00699681 / $22.99
VOL. 44 – JAZZ GREATS ....00699689 / $19.99
VOL. 45 – TV THEMES ....00699718 / $14.95
VOL. 46 – MAINSTREAM ROCK ....00699722 / $16.95
VOL. 47 – JIMI HENDRIX SMASH HITS ....00699723 / $22.99
VOL. 48 – AEROSMITH CLASSICS ....00699724 / $19.99
VOL. 49 – STEVIE RAY VAUGHAN ....00699725 / $19.99
VOL. 50 – VAN HALEN: 1978-1984 ....00110269 / $19.99
VOL. 51 – ALTERNATIVE '90s ....00699727 / $14.99
VOL. 52 – FUNK ....00699728 / $17.99
VOL. 53 – DISCO ....00699729 / $14.99
VOL. 55 – POP METAL ....00699731 / $14.95
VOL. 57 – GUNS 'N' ROSES ....00159922 / $19.99
VOL. 59 – CHET ATKINS ....00702347 / $22.99
VOL. 60 – 3 DOORS DOWN ....00699774 / $14.95
VOL. 62 – CHRISTMAS CAROLS ....00699798 / $12.95
VOL. 63 – CREEDENCE CLEARWATER
           REVIVAL ....00699802 / $17.99
VOL. 64 – ULTIMATE OZZY OSBOURNE ...00699803 / $22.99
VOL. 66 – THE ROLLING STONES ....00699807 / $19.99
VOL. 67 – BLACK SABBATH ....00699808 / $17.99
VOL. 68 – PINK FLOYD –
           DARK SIDE OF THE MOON ....00699809 / $17.99
VOL. 71 – CHRISTIAN ROCK ....00699824 / $14.95

VOL. 74 – SIMPLE STRUMMING SONGS ..00151706 / $19.99
VOL. 75 – TOM PETTY ....00699882 / $19.99
VOL. 76 – COUNTRY HITS ....00699884 / $16.99
VOL. 77 – BLUEGRASS ....00699910 / $17.99
VOL. 78 – NIRVANA ....00700132 / $17.99
VOL. 79 – NEIL YOUNG ....00700133 / $24.99
VOL. 81 – ROCK ANTHOLOGY ....00700176 / $24.99
VOL. 82 – EASY ROCK SONGS ....00700177 / $17.99
VOL. 83 – SUBLIME ....00369114 / $17.99
VOL. 84 – STEELY DAN ....00700200 / $19.99
VOL. 85 – THE POLICE ....00700269 / $17.99
VOL. 86 – BOSTON ....00700465 / $19.99
VOL. 87 – ACOUSTIC WOMEN ....00700763 / $14.99
VOL. 88 – GRUNGE ....00700467 / $16.99
VOL. 89 – REGGAE ....00700468 / $15.99
VOL. 90 – CLASSICAL POP ....00700469 / $14.99
VOL. 91 – BLUES INSTRUMENTALS ......00700505 / $19.99
VOL. 92 – EARLY ROCK
           INSTRUMENTALS ....00700506 / $17.99
VOL. 93 – ROCK INSTRUMENTALS ....00700507 / $17.99
VOL. 94 – SLOW BLUES ....00700508 / $16.99
VOL. 95 – BLUES CLASSICS ....00700509 / $17.99
VOL. 96 – BEST COUNTRY HITS ....00211615 / $16.99
VOL. 97 – CHRISTMAS CLASSICS ....00236542 / $14.99
VOL. 99 – ZZ TOP ....00700762 / $17.99
VOL. 100 – B.B. KING ....00700466 / $17.99
VOL. 101 – SONGS FOR BEGINNERS .....00701917 / $14.99
VOL. 102 – CLASSIC PUNK ....00700769 / $14.99
VOL. 104 – DUANE ALLMAN ....00700846 / $22.99
VOL. 105 – LATIN ....00700939 / $16.99
VOL. 106 – WEEZER ....00700958 / $17.99
VOL. 107 – CREAM ....00701069 / $17.99
VOL. 108 – THE WHO ....00701053 / $17.99
VOL. 109 – STEVE MILLER ....00701054 / $19.99
VOL. 110 – SLIDE GUITAR HITS ....00701055 / $17.99
VOL. 111 – JOHN MELLENCAMP ....00701056 / $14.99
VOL. 112 – QUEEN ....00701052 / $16.99
VOL. 113 – JIM CROCE ....00701058 / $19.99
VOL. 114 – BON JOVI ....00701060 / $17.99
VOL. 115 – JOHNNY CASH ....00701070 / $17.99
VOL. 116 – THE VENTURES ....00701124 / $17.99
VOL. 117 – BRAD PAISLEY ....00701224 / $16.99
VOL. 118 – ERIC JOHNSON ....00701353 / $19.99
VOL. 119 – AC/DC CLASSICS ....00701356 / $19.99
VOL. 120 – PROGRESSIVE ROCK ....00701457 / $14.99
VOL. 121 – U2 ....00701508 / $17.99
VOL. 122 – CROSBY, STILLS & NASH ....00701610 / $16.99
VOL. 123 – LENNON & McCARTNEY
            ACOUSTIC ....00701614 / $16.99
VOL. 124 – SMOOTH JAZZ ....00200664 / $17.99
VOL. 125 – JEFF BECK ....00701687 / $19.99
VOL. 126 – BOB MARLEY ....00701701 / $19.99
VOL. 127 – 1970s ROCK ....00701739 / $17.99
VOL. 129 – MEGADETH ....00701741 / $17.99
VOL. 130 – IRON MAIDEN ....00701742 / $19.99
VOL. 131 – 1990s ROCK ....00701743 / $14.99
VOL. 132 – COUNTRY ROCK ....00701757 / $15.99
VOL. 133 – TAYLOR SWIFT ....00701894 / $16.99
VOL. 135 – MINOR BLUES ....00151350 / $17.99
VOL. 136 – GUITAR THEMES ....00701922 / $14.99
VOL. 137 – IRISH TUNES ....00701966 / $17.99
VOL. 138 – BLUEGRASS CLASSICS ....00701967 / $17.99

VOL. 139 – GARY MOORE ....00702370 / $19.99
VOL. 140 – MORE STEVIE RAY VAUGHAN .00702396 / $24.99
VOL. 141 – ACOUSTIC HITS ....00702401 / $16.99
VOL. 142 – GEORGE HARRISON ....00237697 / $17.99
VOL. 143 – SLASH ....00702425 / $19.99
VOL. 144 – DJANGO REINHARDT ....00702531 / $17.99
VOL. 145 – DEF LEPPARD ....00702532 / $19.99
VOL. 146 – ROBERT JOHNSON ....00702533 / $16.99
VOL. 147 – SIMON & GARFUNKEL ....14041591 / $19.99
VOL. 148 – BOB DYLAN ....14041592 / $17.99
VOL. 149 – AC/DC HITS ....14041593 / $19.99
VOL. 150 – ZAKK WYLDE ....02501717 / $19.99
VOL. 151 – J.S. BACH ....02501730 / $16.99
VOL. 152 – JOE BONAMASSA ....02501751 / $24.99
VOL. 153 – RED HOT CHILI PEPPERS ......00702990 / $22.99
VOL. 155 – ERIC CLAPTON UNPLUGGED .00703085 / $19.99
VOL. 156 – SLAYER ....00703770 / $19.99
VOL. 157 – FLEETWOOD MAC ....00101382 / $17.99
VOL. 159 – WES MONTGOMERY ....00102593 / $22.99
VOL. 160 – T-BONE WALKER ....00102641 / $17.99
VOL. 161 – THE EAGLES ACOUSTIC ....00102659 / $19.99
VOL. 162 – THE EAGLES HITS ....00102667 / $19.99
VOL. 163 – PANTERA ....00103036 / $19.99
VOL. 164 – VAN HALEN: 1986-1995 ....00110270 / $19.99
VOL. 165 – GREEN DAY ....00210343 / $17.99
VOL. 166 – MODERN BLUES ....00700764 / $16.99
VOL. 167 – DREAM THEATER ....00111938 / $24.99
VOL. 168 – KISS ....00113421 / $17.99
VOL. 170 – THREE DAYS GRACE ....00117337 / $16.99
VOL. 171 – JAMES BROWN ....00117420 / $16.99
VOL. 172 – THE DOOBIE BROTHERS ....00119670 / $17.99
VOL. 173 – TRANS-SIBERIAN
            ORCHESTRA ....00119907 / $19.99
VOL. 174 – SCORPIONS ....00122119 / $19.99
VOL. 175 – MICHAEL SCHENKER ....00122127 / $19.99
VOL. 176 – BLUES BREAKERS WITH JOHN
            MAYALL & ERIC CLAPTON ......00122132 / $19.99
VOL. 177 – ALBERT KING ....00123271 / $17.99
VOL. 178 – JASON MRAZ ....00124165 / $17.99
VOL. 179 – RAMONES ....00127073 / $17.99
VOL. 180 – BRUNO MARS ....00129706 / $16.99
VOL. 181 – JACK JOHNSON ....00129854 / $16.99
VOL. 182 – SOUNDGARDEN ....00138161 / $17.99
VOL. 183 – BUDDY GUY ....00138240 / $17.99
VOL. 184 – KENNY WAYNE SHEPHERD ...00138258 / $17.99
VOL. 185 – JOE SATRIANI ....00139457 / $17.99
VOL. 186 – GRATEFUL DEAD ....00139459 / $17.99
VOL. 187 – JOHN DENVER ....00140839 / $19.99
VOL. 188 – MÖTLEY CRÜE ....00141145 / $19.99
VOL. 189 – JOHN MAYER ....00144350 / $22.99
VOL. 190 – DEEP PURPLE ....00146152 / $19.99
VOL. 191 – PINK FLOYD CLASSICS ....00146164 / $17.99
VOL. 192 – JUDAS PRIEST ....00151352 / $19.99
VOL. 193 – STEVE VAI ....00156028 / $19.99
VOL. 195 – METALLICA: 1983-1988 ....00234291 / $24.99
VOL. 196 – METALLICA: 1991-2016 ....00234292 / $22.99

Prices, contents, and availability subject to change without notice.

HAL•LEONARD®
www.halleonard.com

0423
173